UPDATED EDITION

Guess What!

Workbook 6

with Digital Pack

T0343045

American English

Susan Rivers

Series Editor: Lesley Koustaff

Shaftesbury Road, Cambridge CB2 8EA, United Kingdom

One Liberty Plaza, 20th Floor, New York, NY 10006, USA

477 Williamstown Road, Port Melbourne, VIC 3207, Australia

314–321, 3rd Floor, Plot 3, Splendor Forum, Jasola District Centre, New Delhi – 110025, India

103 Penang Road, #05–06/07, Visioncrest Commercial, Singapore 238467

Cambridge University Press & Assessment is a department of the University of Cambridge.

We share the University's mission to contribute to society through the pursuit of education, learning and research at the highest international levels of excellence.

www.cambridge.org
Information on this title: www.cambridge.org/9781009798617

First published 2016
Updated edition 2024

20 19 18 17 16 15 14 13 12 11 10 9 8 7 6 5 4 3 2 1

Printed in Malaysia by Vivar Printing

A catalogue record for this publication is available from the British Library

ISBN 978-1-009-79861-7   Workbook with Digital Pack Level 6
ISBN 978-1-009-48242-4   Student's Book with eBook Level 6
ISBN 978-1-009-79891-4   Teacher's Book with Digital Pack Level 6

Additional resources for this publication at www.cambridge.org/guesswhatue

Contents

Seasons and weather

1 **Read and complete the sentences.**

1 It rains every day in ___monsoon___ season.

2 There isn't any rain in a _____ .

3 _____ is colder than fall.

4 A lot of plants and flowers start to grow in _____ .

5 We can often see lightning and hear _____ in a _____ .

2 (Think) **Circle the one that doesn't belong.**

1 summer   (storm)   fall
2 winter   flood   drought
3 thunder   monsoon   lightning

3 **Read and write the words. Then number the pictures.**

1 This is the hottest season.   ___summer___

2 This is the coldest season.   _____

3 This is when it rains too much, and there's water in the streets
and buildings.   _____

4 Leaves change color and fall from the trees in this season.   _____

5 This is the light we see in the sky in a storm.   _____

6 This is when it doesn't rain for a long time, and the land is very dry.   _____

a

b   1

c

d

e

f

My picture dictionary ➔ Go to page 84: Write the new words.

4 **Read and circle the correct words.**

1 There _____ rain, but there _____ any thunder or lightning.

   a (was, wasn't)   b did, didn't

2 _____ they play soccer in the rain? Yes, they _____ .

   a Were, were   b Did, did

3 Pablo _____ go windsurfing because it _____ windy.

   a wasn't, didn't   b didn't, wasn't

4 _____ your vacation fun? No, it _____ .

   a Was, wasn't   b Did, didn't

5 Maria _____ enjoy her vacation because there _____ a lot of storms.

   a weren't, did   b didn't, were

5 **Complete the questions and answers.**

1 Where _____did_____ Anna go on summer vacation? She _____ to Bali with her cousin, Claire.

2 What _____ the weather like? It _____ hot and sunny.

3 What _____ they do? They _____ to the beach every day.

4 _____ there sharks in the ocean? No, there _____ , but there _____ dolphins.

Anna and Claire's summer vacation

6 **Look at activity 5. Write the questions.**

1 _Did Anna go to Bali for a spring vacation?_

   No, she didn't. She went during the summer vacation.

2 _____

   No, it wasn't. It was hot and sunny.

3 _____

   Yes, they did. They went every day.

4 _____

   Yes, there were. There were a lot of dolphins.

5 _____

   Yes, it was. It was a lot of fun!

7 **Join the two sentences using *when*.**

1 The students were excited. They visited the museum.
   The students were excited when they visited the museum.

2 Gemma's grandmother moved. She felt sad.
   _____
   _____

3 The weather was awful. Luke and Kate arrived.
   _____

4 Peter saw the bat. He was scared.
   _____

5 My father went to India. He lost his cell phone.
   _____

8 **Put the words in order.**

1 was / storm / yesterday. / There / a
   There was a storm yesterday.

2 saw / happy / Lisa / when / was / her cousins. / she
   _____

3 rock climbing / didn't / Karen / go / last week.
   _____

4 Juan / ten, / was / When / went / he / to Brazil.
   _____

5 floods / were / There / my town / last month. / in
   _____

9 **My World Complete the sentences about you.**

1 When I was five, _____ .

2 I felt happy when _____ .

3 When _____ , I felt sad.

10 **Read the story again. Circle the correct words and then number.**

☐ **a** Jack and Ruby are **surprised** / **happy** to help Sofia with the island game.

☐ **b** Ruby wants to go back to the house because there's a **storm** / **flood**.

☐ **c** Sofia wants to **enter** / **watch** a computer game competition.

1 **d** Jack is surprised to see (**Sofia**) / **Ruby**.

11 **Read and match the questions and answers.**

1 Who is Jack surprised to see? `C`   **a** Yes, they do.

2 What does Sofia want to enter? ☐   **b** No, it isn't.

3 Do Jack and Ruby want to help her? ☐   **c** Sofia.

4 Is the game finished? ☐   **d** Because there's a dangerous storm.

5 Why is Ruby scared? ☐   **e** A computer game competition.

12 **What can you do to show the value: ask your friends for help?**

1 You can ask a friend for help with your homework.

2 _____

3 _____

Skills: *Reading*

13 Read Tom's article in the Pineville school newsletter. Complete with the past tense of the words in the box.

~~is~~   isn't   are   rain   go   help   start   arrive   stay   see

Bad storm hits Pineville!
By Tom Banks

There ¹___*was*___ a dangerous storm in Pineville last Sunday night. It ²_____ at 9:00 p.m. At first, it was very windy, and there was a lot of thunder and lightning. Then it ³_____ for a long time. There ⁴_____ floods at the Pineville Shopping Mall and the bus station. A lot of trees fell down. The police ⁵_____ people get home. It was very scary.

When the teachers, Mr. Jones and Ms. Green, ⁶_____ at our school on Monday morning, they were surprised. They ⁷_____ water in our cafeteria, and there was a big tree in the library! The teachers had to leave the school because it ⁸_____ safe. The Pineville students ⁹_____ at home last Monday, but they ¹⁰_____ back to school last Tuesday. The library is closed until next week. What a mess!

14 Read and write *true* or *false*.

1   The storm started at 8:00 p.m. last Sunday night.   _*false*_

2   There was thunder, lightning, and a lot of wind.   _____

3   The Pineville Shopping Mall fell down.   _____

4   There was a flood in the bus station.   _____

5   The teachers had to stay in the school.   _____

6   The Pineville students didn't go to school on Monday.   _____

15 **TIP** **A noun is a word that names a person, place, or thing.**
Tom Banks lives in *Pineville*. There was *a storm*.
Read Tom's article again. Circle six examples of nouns.

Skills: *Writing*

16 **Make notes about a weather event in your town.**

Weather event:		
Where:		
When:		
What happened:	1	
	2	
	3	
	4	
	5	

17 **Write an article about a weather event in your town.**

Title: _____

_____

_____

_____

_____

_____

_____

_____

_____

_____

What do the shadows in a painting tell us?

1 **Read and match.**

1   We see short shadows .... `d`

2   Shadows are long ....

3   Artists paint shadows on the right ....

4   The shadows are on the left ....

5   In winter paintings, we often ....

a   when the Sun is on the right.

b   when the light comes from the side.

c   when the Sun is on the left.

d   when the light comes from above.

e   see long shadows.

2 **Circle the shadow in the two drawings. Then answer the questions.**

1   Where's the shadow in each picture?
    In picture a, it's on the right of the tree.

2   Where's the Sun in each picture?

3   Is the shadow in each picture long or short?

4   What season is it in each picture?

3 **In your notebook, draw and write about the things you can see outside and their shadows.**

Evaluation

 1 Look at Lisa's diary. Then read and circle the correct words.

Lisa's spring diary

Sunday	Monday	Tuesday	Wednesday	Thursday	Friday	Saturday
Snowy	Sunny and cold *Spring vacation	Cloudy and warmer	Thunder and lightning storms *Arrived in Florida!	Rain and wind	Rain and wind	Flood! *Left Florida!

This is Lisa's ¹(spring)/ summer diary. It ²was / were cold on Sunday and Monday. Lisa and her family ³were / went to Florida on Wednesday. When they arrived, there was an awful ⁴drought / storm. They had to leave Florida because there was a ⁵flood / rain.

2 Look at activity 1. Answer the questions.

1 What was the weather like on Monday?

It was sunny and cold on Monday.

2 Did Lisa visit Florida in the winter?

_____

3 What was the weather like when they arrived in Florida?

_____

4 What was the weather like on Thursday?

_____

5 Was there a drought in Florida?

_____

6 Did Lisa enjoy her vacation?

_____

3 Complete the sentences about this unit.

✓ = I can …   ✗ = I can't …

☐ **1** … name four seasons.

☐ **2** … talk about dangerous weather.

☐ **3** … talk and ask about things that happened in the past.

☐ **4** … talk about two things that happened at the same time using *when*.

☐ **5** … talk about asking a friend for help.

6 The part of this unit I found the most interesting was _____ .

1 Camping

1 Read and write *true* or *false*.

1 A backpack helps us see at night. _____false_____

2 We can keep warm with a blanket. _____

3 People usually drink coffee from a bowl. _____

4 We can sleep in a sleeping bag when we don't have a bed. _____

5 People usually eat pizza from a cup. _____

2 Think Read and write the words.

~~sleeping bag~~   bowl   backpack   flashlight   water bottle   plate   tent   cup

1 Things we can open and close

_____sleeping bag_____   _____   _____   _____

2 Things we use for eating and drinking

_____   _____   _____   _____

3 Things we usually use at night

_____   _____   _____

3 My World Which camping things do you have? Complete the sentences.

1 I have _____.

2 I don't have _____.

My picture dictionary ➡ Go to page 85: Write the new words.

4 Read and complete the sentences. Use the words in parentheses.

1 Sam ___wanted to go___ camping with his class last month. (want / go)

2 He _____ early that morning, but he forgot to set his alarm clock. (need / get up)

3 Then he forgot his sleeping bag, so he _____ home and get it. (have / run)

4 He _____ very fast to the bus stop, but he was too late. (try / run)

5 His mom _____ him to the campsite. (have / drive)

5 Put the words in order.

1 go / Maria / to / mountain biking. / and / wanted / her family

Maria and her family wanted to go mountain biking.

2 the / take / camping trip. / a sleeping bag / forgot / My brother / to / on

_____

3 this / bed / I / to / my / had / make / morning.

_____

4 their / do / needed / The students / to / homework / last night.

_____

5 was / started / The baby / tired. / because / to / she / cry

_____

6 Complete the sentences about you. Use the words in the box.

> want   need   have

1 I _____ yesterday.

2 I _____ last night.

3 I _____ this morning.

7 Look at the chart. Then answer the questions.

Ms. Lee's Grade 6 Class To-Do list

sweep the floor	water the plants	collect the books	clean the classroom	wash the cups	turn off the computers
Diego Anna	Sam Ellie	Ben Joe	Hae Akoi	Harry Olivia	Elena Leila

1   What did Ms. Lee ask Ben to do?

She asked him to collect the books.

2   What did she ask Elena to do?

_____

3   What did she ask Sam and Ellie to do?

_____

4   What did she ask Harry to do?

_____

5   What did she ask Anna to do?

_____

8 Look at activity 7. Write the questions.

1   _What did Ms. Lee ask Olivia to do?_

She asked her to wash the cups.

2   _____

She asked them to clean the classroom.

3   _____

She asked him to sweep the floor.

4   _____

She asked them to collect the books.

5   _____

She asked her to water the plants.

9 (Think) **Read the story again. Correct the mistakes and then number.**

☐ **a** The children make tents with sleeping bags and camp in the forest. _____

☐ **b** The naughty ants are trying to show them something. _____

1 **c** Ruby, Jack, and Sofia are on an island in Sofia's ~~book~~. _____*game*_____

☐ **d** They find a photograph of the island. _____

10 **Read and circle the correct answers.**

1 Where are the children?
   a They're at home.   **b** (They're on an island.)

2 What are the ants doing?
   a They're showing the children a map.   **b** They're showing the children the island.

3 Where is the map?
   a It's in a tree.   **b** It's in a tent.

4 Do the children have tents in their backpacks?
   a Yes, they do.   **b** No, they don't.

5 What do they use to make tents?
   a They use blankets.   **b** They use maps.

11 **What can you do to show the value: be resourceful?**

1 _You can use a stick to get something_ _out of water._

2 You can use the Internet to _____ _____

3 You can use _____ to _____

Skills: *Reading*

12 **Read and complete the story. Use the words in parentheses.**

Carol is a smart girl, but she always forgets things. One day, she went hiking in the jungle. It ¹ _started_ (start) to rain. She ² _____ (forget) to ³ _____ (take) an umbrella, so she ⁴ _____ (have) to use a big leaf to keep dry. Then she got very thirsty. She forgot ⁵ _____ (take) her water bottle, so she ⁶ _____ (have) to ⁷ _____ (use) her hat to get water from a waterfall. She was tired. She ⁸ _____ (forget) to take a sleeping bag, so she ⁹ _____ (need) to ¹⁰ _____ (put) her blanket between two trees. She tried ¹¹ _____ (go) home, but she ¹² _____ (get) lost because she didn't have a map. She ¹³ _____ (need) to go west, so she ¹⁴ _____ (look) at the Sun to find her way home. Carol is a very smart girl!

13 **Look at activity 12. Read and complete the sentences.**

> Carol forgot to take _an umbrella_ . → She used _a big leaf_ .

> She forgot to take _____ . → She used _____ .

> She forgot to take _____ . → She used _____ .

> She forgot to take _____ . → She used _____ .

14 **(TIP)** **A verb is an action word. *Is*, *are*, and *am* are verbs, too.**
I *forgot* my umbrella when I *went* out. I *got* wet because it *was raining*.
Read Carol's story again. Circle six examples of verbs in the story.

Skills: *Writing*

15 Imagine a story about someone being resourceful. Make notes about what he/she did.

> Where was he/she? _____

> What did he/she forget to take?   →   What did he/she use?
> _____   _____

> What did he/she forget to take?   →   What did he/she use?
> _____   _____

> What did he/she forget to take?   →   What did he/she use?
> _____   _____

16 Write a story about someone being resourceful.

_____
_____
_____
_____
_____
_____
_____
_____
_____
_____
_____

How do we estimate measurements?

1 Match the pictures to the questions. Then match the questions and answers.

1 How much orange juice is there? [c]   a There's about 5 liters.

2 How heavy is the backpack? [ ]   b It's about 6 kilograms.

3 How long is the flashlight? [ ]   c There's about 100 milliliters.

4 How much water is there? [ ]   d It's about 20 centimeters.

2 This line shows the numbers 0–100 divided into tens. Estimate where the numbers in the box are on the line.

3 Estimate which numbers the arrows are pointing to on these lines.

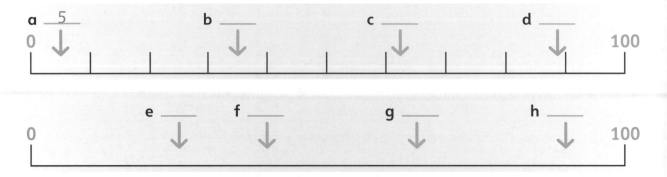

Evaluation

  Look at Mr. Wood's to-do list. Complete the Venn diagram.

Mr. Wood's to-do list	Andy	Sara	Tim	Pam	Dan
collect the flashlights		✓	✓		
put up the tents	✓	✓		✓	✓
wash the bowls			✓	✓	
cook the dinner		✓	✓		✓
dry the cups and plates	✓	✓		✓	✓
put away the blankets	✓		✓		✓

Dan   **Both**   **Tim**

put up the tents _____ _____

_____ _____ _____

2 **Look at activity 1. Write the sentences.**

1   Mr. Wood / ask / Sara and Tim

Mr. Wood asked Sara and Tim to collect the flashlights.

2   have to / the blankets

_____

3   Mr. Wood / ask / Tim and Pam

_____

4   have to / the tents

_____

3 **Complete the sentences about this unit.**

✓ = I can …   ✗ = I can't …

☐ 1 … name ten camping things.

☐ 2 … talk about what people *needed to, forgot to, tried to, had to* do.

☐ 3 … ask and answer *What did … ask … to do?* questions.

☐ 4 … talk about being resourceful.

☐ 5 … write a story about being resourceful.

6   The part of this unit I need to practice is _____ .

2 Talent show

1 (Think) **Write the words. Then number the pictures.**

1　l y p a   t t i s n n u m r e s 　　＿＿＿*play instruments*＿＿＿
2　g l j e u g 　　＿＿＿＿＿＿＿＿＿＿＿
3　d a e r   t e r o y p 　　＿＿＿＿＿＿＿＿＿＿＿
4　t p i n a   a i r o s t r t p 　　＿＿＿＿＿＿＿＿＿＿＿
5　k e a m   l p u t u c r s e s 　　＿＿＿＿＿＿＿＿＿＿＿
6　o d   k s r t c i 　　＿＿＿＿＿＿＿＿＿＿＿

a ［1］   b ［ ］   c ［ ］   d ［ ］   e ［ ］   f ［ ］

2 (Think) **Complete the chart. Use the words in the box.**

> ~~tell jokes~~　do acrobatics　do street dancing
> do tricks　play instruments　do cartwheels

Things people can do sitting down	Things people can't do sitting down
tell jokes	＿＿＿＿＿＿＿
＿＿＿＿＿＿＿	＿＿＿＿＿＿＿
＿＿＿＿＿＿＿	＿＿＿＿＿＿＿

3 (My World) **Complete the sentences about your friends and family.**

1　＿＿＿＿＿＿＿＿＿ is good at telling jokes.

2　＿＿＿＿＿＿＿＿＿ is good at playing an instrument.

3　＿＿＿＿＿＿＿＿＿ is good at ＿＿＿＿＿＿＿＿ .

My picture dictionary ➜ Go to page 86: Write the new words.

4 Look and complete the sentences.

1 Sandra is _____*better than*_____ Jen at street dancing.

2 Dave is _____ at doing cartwheels.

3 Tom is _____ Sue at playing a musical instrument.

4 Tim is _____ at street dancing.

5 Matt is _____ than Joe at doing cartwheels.

5 Look at activity 4. Write the sentences.

1 *Jen is the worst at street dancing.* _____ (Jen / street dancing)

2 _____ (Joe / Dave / do cartwheels)

3 _____ (Bea / play a musical instrument)

4 _____ (Sandra / Tim / street dancing)

5 _____ (Tom / play a musical instrument)

6 My World Complete the chart about you and a friend. Then write sentences.

	Better	Worse
Me		
My friend		

1 *I'm better than my friend at* _____ .

2 I'm worse _____ .

3 My friend _____ .

4 _____

7 Look and answer the questions.

1 Who's better at reading poetry, Pete or Liam? _____Liam is._____

2 Who's the worst at making sculptures? _____

3 Who's better at painting portraits, Bob or Eva? _____

4 Who's the best at reading poetry? _____

5 Who's worse at making sculptures, Jake or Nadia? _____

8 Look at activity 7 and write the questions. Use the words in parentheses.

1 _Who's the best at making sculptures?_ _____ (best)
George is.

2 _____ (worse / Bob / Rosa)
Rosa is.

3 _____ (worst)
Cindy is.

4 _____ (better / Nadia / Nick)
Nadia is.

5 _____ (best)
Oliver is.

9 Read and complete.

Paula: You're very good at street dancing, Clara.

Clara: Thanks, but I'm not the ¹_____best_____ in my family. My brother, Lucas, is ²_____ than me.

Paula: Who's ³_____ at doing cartwheels, you or your brother?

Clara: My brother ⁴_____ . He's very good, but he's ⁵_____ than me at doing acrobatics.

Paula: ⁶_____ the best in your family at playing sports?

Clara: My sister ⁷_____ . She plays basketball every Saturday morning.

Paula: Do you go with her?

Clara: No, I don't. I'm the ⁸_____ in my family at waking up early. I always want to sleep!

10 **Read the story again. Circle the correct words and then number.**

1 The children follow _____ to the canoe.
  a an animal   **b** (some footprints)   **c** the map

Jack stops the canoe safely away from the _____ .
  a hippos   **b** crocodiles   **c** fish

Jack tries to slow the _____ down.
  a river   **b** canoe   **c** hippos

They get in the canoe with the _____ and the compass.
  a map   **b** tent   **c** river

11 **Read and correct the sentences.**

1 The children follow the very small footprints.
The children follow the very big footprints.

2 Jack finds the compass in a canoe.
_____

3 Sofia is the worst at reading the map.
_____

4 The children follow the river south.
_____

5 The children are scared of the fish in the water.
_____

12 **Write about two ways you showed the value: work together.**

1 *My sister and I made dinner together.*

2 _____

3 _____

Story   Value   **23**

Skills: *Reading*

13 Read Emily's email. Circle the correct words.

Hello Grandma,

I want to tell you about my new friend, Zoey. I met Zoey last month at dance class. We like going hiking together. We like going shopping together, too. We do everything together! We're both friendly and talkative. We're both very smart, too! Zoey's very artistic. She's ¹(**better**)/ **best** at painting and making sculptures than I am, but I'm sportier than she is. I'm ²**good** / **better** at doing cartwheels and skateboarding than she is.

I'm ³**better** / **best** at playing musical instruments, too. We had a talent show at school. The teacher asked Zoey and me to play the piano. When we played at the show, everyone was surprised! Zoey was the ⁴**better** / **best**, not me. Why? Zoey is more hardworking than I am. She practiced every day, but I didn't. I went skateboarding and rock climbing. I watched TV and played video games, too. I was happy for her. Now I know that if you want to be the ⁵**best** / **good**, you have to work hard!

Love,

Emily

14 Look at activity 13. Read and write *true* or *false*.

1   Emily met Zoey at singing class.   *false*

2   Zoey is better at painting than Emily.   _____

3   Emily is better at making sculptures than Zoey.   _____

4   Emily practiced the piano every day but Zoey didn't.   _____

5   Emily thinks that having fun is more important than
    working hard if you want to be the best.   _____

15 (Think) Complete the chart. Use the words in the box.

> more artistic   smart   ~~sportier~~   friendly
> better at skateboarding   better at painting

Emily	Zoey	Both
sportier	_____	_____
_____	_____	_____

16 (TIP) **An adjective is a word that describes nouns.**

Emily and Zoey are *friendly*.   The park is *big*.   The pencil is *new*.

Read Emily's email again. Circle the examples of adjectives.

Skills: *Writing*

17 **Make notes about you and a friend.**

My friend's name: _____

Where we met: _____

Things we like doing together: _____

Adjectives to describe us:

Me

Both

My friend

_____   _____   _____

_____   _____   _____

18 **Write an email about you and your friend.**

Hello _____ ,

_____

_____

_____

_____

_____

_____

_____

_____

Love,

_____

What abilities do we need for physical activities?

1 **Read and circle the correct words.**

1 Some acrobats need **strength** / **speed** to lift other acrobats up in the air.
2 Runners and swimmers need **balance** / **speed** to win a race.
3 When we climb high mountains, we need **speed** / **stamina** to help us.
4 Ballet dancers and gymnasts need good **stamina** / **balance** to stand on one leg.

2 **Write sentences about what we need for these physical activities.**

1 *When we do cartwheels, we need balance.*

2 _____

3 _____

4 _____

5 _____

6 _____

3 **Think of three physical activities you do. For each activity, write what you need: speed, strength, stamina, or balance.**

1 When I _____ , I need _____ .

2 _____

3 _____

Evaluation

1 **Look and complete the sentences.**

Joe   Kevin   Tina

Frank   Mark
Penny

Simon
Anna   Sarah

1 Tina ___is worse at___
___making sculptures___
than Kevin.

2 Joe is the _____
_____ making sculptures.

3 Frank _____
_____
than Penny.

4 Mark _____
_____ .

5 Sarah _____
_____
than Simon.

6 Anna _____
_____ .

2 **Complete the questions and answers.**

1 _____Who's better_____ at doing tricks, Mr. Lee or Mr. Jones?

Mr. Jones _____ . He's very good.

2 _____ at reading poetry?

Jimmy _____ . He's not good at all.

3 _____ at telling jokes, your father or _____ ?

My mother _____ . She's really funny.

4 _____ at painting portraits?

Olivia _____ . Her portraits are beautiful.

5 _____ at doing cartwheels, _____ or your friend?

I _____ . I always fall down!

3 **Complete the sentences about this unit.**

✓ = I can …   ✗ = I can't …

☐ **1** … name ten talent show activities.

☐ **2** … compare using *better*, *best*, *worse*, and *worst*.

☐ **3** … ask and answer questions comparing people.

☐ **4** … talk about working together.

☐ **5** … write an email comparing people.

6 The part of this unit I found the most useful was _____ .

Review Units 1 and 2

1 (Think) **Read and complete the word puzzle and find the secret word.**

1 This helps us find places.
2 This is bad weather. Sometimes there's rain, thunder, and lightning.
3 This is a quick light in the sky.
4 This helps us see in the dark.
5 This is when there's no rain.
6 This is when there is too much water in streets and buildings.
7 We put this around bodies to keep warm.

	1		
	m	a	p

The secret word is _____

2 **Write sentences. Use the correct form of the verbs.**

1 when / Kevin / arrive / Florida / start / rain

   When Kevin arrived in Florida, it started to rain.

2 John / forget / take / map / last weekend

   _____

3 there / is / flood / last spring

   _____

4 Larry / better / tell jokes / Henry

   _____

5 Ms. Hill / ask / students / wash / cups / yesterday

   _____

6 who / worse / make sculptures / Jean / Sam?

   _____

3 (Think) **Circle the one that doesn't belong.**

1 backpack   sleeping bag   drought
2 winter   summer   storm
3 do street dancing read poetry   tell jokes
4 thunder   fall   lightning
5 do acrobatics   paint portraits   do cartwheels
6 flashlight   water bottle   cup

28

4 **Read and write the names.**

My name's Justin. Yesterday, my friends and I did a talent show. It was great! I told jokes because my friends say that I'm funny. Kat is the best at playing musical instruments. She played the guitar and sang. Eva read poetry, Andy did acrobatics, and Fraser juggled. Paula is artistic. She painted a portrait of me!

Before the show, everyone was very nervous. We all talked a lot. Can you guess who said these sentences?

1 I need to find my book of poems. _____Eva_____

2 Oh, no! I forgot to bring my paintbrush! _____

3 I have to make people laugh! _____

4 I don't want to drop the balls. _____

5 I need to have good balance. _____

6 Shh! I'm trying to practice my song. _____

5 **Answer the questions about you.**

1 Was there a drought in your country last summer?

_____

2 What do you need to do after school tomorrow?

_____

3 What did your mom ask you to do yesterday?

_____

4 Who is the worst at telling jokes in your family?

_____

5 Who is the best at doing cartwheels in your class?

_____

International food

1 **Complete the words. Then check (✓) the correct ingredients.**

1 I like s t e w.

a ✓

b

c ✓

2 I don't like _ u _ _ i.

a

b

c

3 I'd like to try _ oo _ _ e _ .

a

b

c

4 I often eat _ i _ _ a _ _ _ _ i _ _ .

a

b

c

2 **Read and write the words.**

1 These are from China. They're made with flour, meat, and vegetables. _dumplings_

2 This food is from India. Sometimes it's yellow. It's made with meat and vegetables. _____

3 This food is from Mexico. It's made with flour, meat, cheese, and vegetables. _____

4 This food is from Spain. It has rice, vegetables, and meat or fish. _____

5 This food is from Greece. It's made from meat and vegetables. _____

3 **Which food is your country famous for? Name two.**

1 My country is famous for _____ .

2 It's famous for _____ , too.

My picture dictionary ➜ **Go to page 87: Write the new words.**

4 **Write sentences.**

1 I / my mom / make noodles for lunch / today

I want my mom to make noodles for lunch today.

2 Pablo / Ray / play soccer / yesterday

3 Our teacher / us / speak English / every day

4 Helen's dad / her / try / dumplings / last night

5 Jenny / Greg / play volleyball / every afternoon

5 **Read and correct the sentences.**

1 I wanted my mom to (made) some noodles.

I wanted my mom to make some noodles.

2 She wanted Zak try a kebab.

3 My sister wanted we to buy fish and chips.

4 Rick want me to make rice and beans for dinner.

5 We wanted our dad to bought tacos for lunch.

6 **What do your mom and dad want you to do? Write two things.**

1 My mom _____ .

2 My dad _____ .

7 Read and complete the sentences. Use the words in parentheses.

1 I _____went_____ to the supermarket ____to buy____ some rice. (go / buy)

2 I _____ some rice _____ some sushi. (buy / make)

3 I _____ some sushi _____ to a party. (make / take)

4 My friend Tina _____ a cake _____ our friend, Jake. (bake / give)

5 We all _____ to the party _____ a good time. (go / have)

8 Look and write sentences.

JAKE'S TO-DO LIST
- ✓ Call friends – invite them for dinner
- ✓ Go to the bookstore – buy a recipe book
- ✓ Go to the market – buy meat
- ✓ Buy flour – make dumplings
- ✓ Make a cake – have for dessert

LAURA'S TO-DO LIST
- ✓ Catch a bus – go to town
- ✓ Go to the park – meet Anna
- ✓ Take a ball – play soccer
- ✓ Go to the store – buy juice and chips
- ✓ Go home – watch TV

1 Laura / buy juice and chips
   Laura went to the store to buy juice and chips.

2 Jake / buy a recipe book
   _____

3 Laura / watch TV
   _____

4 Jake / buy meat
   _____

9 Look at activity 8. Answer the questions.

1 Why did Laura catch a bus?
   She caught a bus to go to town.

2 Why did Jake make a cake?
   _____

3 Why did Jake buy flour?
   _____

4 Why did Laura take a ball to the park?
   _____

5 Why did Jake call his friends?
   _____

10 **Read the story again. Match and then number.**

1	The children are hungry, but they __c__	**a** the yeti and forget the map and compass.
	They run away from ____	**b** vegetables, and they cook an omelette.
	They find another ____	**c** can't take the bird's eggs.
	They find more ____	**d** egg close to some onions.

11 **Answer the questions.**

1 Can the children take the animals' eggs?

No, they can't.

2 What do they find in the basket?

_____

3 Do they find some fruit?

_____

4 What do they cook?

_____

5 What do they forget?

_____

12 **Think of four kinds of food you usually eat to show the value: eat healthy food.**

1 _I usually eat an apple at lunchtime._

2 _____

3 _____

4 _____

5 _____

Story Value **33**

Skills: *Reading*

13 **Read Steph's food blog. Then number the photographs.**

Steph the Chef

Last night, my family and I went to my grandmother's house to enjoy a family dinner. Grandma wanted me to help her cook (because I'm Steph the Chef, of course!). We cooked a wonderful American dish called Macaroni Cheese. It's one of my favorite dishes. I want to share the recipe with you today.

Chef Steph's Grandma's Easy, Cheesy Macaroni Cheese

1 box of pasta	Cook the pasta for 8 minutes. Mix the egg and milk. Add butter and cheese to the egg and milk. Put the pasta in a baking dish. Pour the egg, milk, butter, and cheese mixture on the pasta. Bake at 175 degrees for 30 to 40 minutes until the top is golden brown.
1 egg	
2 cups of milk	
2 tablespoons of butter	
2½ cups of cheese	Mmmm. Serve the pasta with vegetables or a salad for an easy, delicious meal. Enjoy!

a

b

c

d

e 1

14 **Look at activity 13. Answer the questions.**

1 Where did Steph and her family go?
They went to Steph's grandmother's house.

2 What did Steph's grandmother want her to do?
_____

3 What did they make?
_____

4 Is it difficult to make?
_____

5 What ingredients are in the recipe?
_____

15 **(TIP)** **When giving instructions, don't use *you*. Start the sentence with a verb.**
✗ You mix the egg and the milk.
✓ Mix the egg and the milk.
Read Steph's blog again. Underline three sentences that give instructions.

Skills: *Writing*

16   Make notes about a recipe you like. Write the ingredients you need and then number the ingredients in the order you use them.

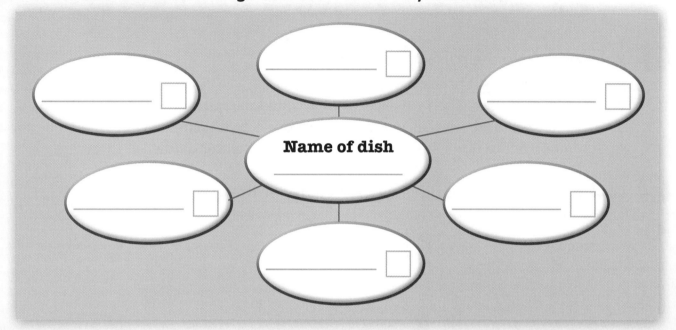

Name of dish

17   Write a food blog and include a recipe.

Why is it important to drink water?

1 **Read and circle the correct words.**

1 Some / (Most) / All of the brain is water.

2 The water we lose when we're very hot is called **perspiration** / **blood** / **skin**.

3 When we don't drink water, we sometimes have **a toothache** / **an earache** / **a headache**.

4 It's important to drink **4–6** / **6–8** / **8–10** glasses of water a day.

2 **Look at the bar chart and line graph. Answer the questions.**

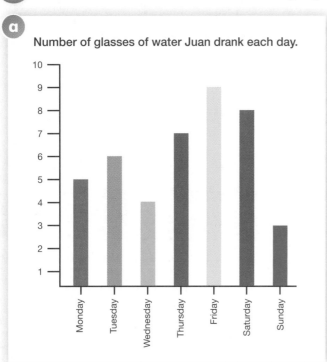

Number of glasses of water Juan drank each day.

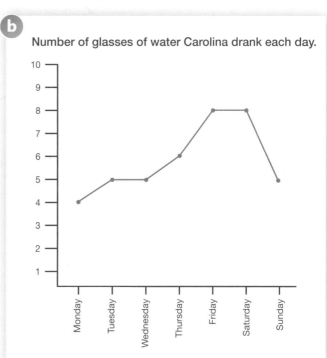

Number of glasses of water Carolina drank each day.

1 Who drank five glasses of water on Sunday? _____Carolina_____

2 Which day did Juan drink the most water? _____

3 Which day did Carolina drink six glasses of water? _____

4 Which day did the children drink the same number of glasses of water? _____

5 Who drank the most water this week? _____

3 **Look at activity 2. Write questions and ask a friend.**

1 Who drank _____ glasses of water on _____ ?

2 How many glasses of water _____ ?

3 _____

Evaluation

1 **Read and match.**

1 Ethan went to an Indian restaurant   `b`   **a** to learn to make kebabs.

2 Olivia bought rice   ☐   **b** to have curry.

3 Sandra went to a Greek cooking class   ☐   **c** to put in the tacos.

4 Oscar went to the supermarket   ☐   **d** to buy meat and vegetables for the stew.

5 Seth bought potatoes   ☐   **e** to make sushi.

6 Miguel cooked the meat   ☐   **f** to make fish and chips.

2 **Read and circle the correct answers.**

1 My mom wanted me to _____ .
   a made my bed   **b** (make my bed)

2 The boy went to the park _____ .
   a to go skateboarding   **b** to went skateboarding

3 Paul wanted his sister _____ .
   a make tacos for dinner   **b** to make tacos for dinner

4 My dad bought some flowers _____ .
   a to give to my mom   **b** to gave to my mom

5 The teacher wants her students to _____ .
   a study hard   **b** studied hard

6 May made dumplings and noodles _____ .
   a to took to the party   **b** to take to the party

7 My grandparents wanted us to _____ .
   a visit them last summer   **b** visited them last summer

3 **Complete the sentences about this unit.**

✓ = I can …   ✗ = I can't …

☐ 1 … name ten international foods.

☐ 2 … talk about people wanting someone to do something.

☐ 3 … talk about why someone did something using *to*.

☐ 4 … talk about eating healthy food.

☐ 5 … write a food blog with a recipe.

6 The part of this unit I enjoyed the most was _____ .

1 Think **Look and write the words.**

electric guitar   keyboard   flute   violin   ~~clarinet~~   trombone

1

Scott can play the

_____clarinet_____ .

2

Amy can play the

_____ .

3

Kai can play the

_____ .

4

Maria can play the

_____ .

5

Josh can play the

_____ .

6

Amelia can play the

_____ .

2 Think **Circle the one that doesn't belong.**

1   trumpet   saxophone   (keyboard)
2   violin   trombone   electric guitar
3   flute   cymbals   drums
4   clarinet   violin   flute

3 My World **What's your favorite and least favorite instrument?**

1   My favorite _____ .

2   My least favorite _____ .

My picture dictionary ➜ Go to page 88: Write the new words.

4 Complete the chart.

Adjective	Adverb
loud	_____
quiet	_____
good	_____
bad	_____
beautiful	_____
quick	_____

5 Look and write sentences. Use the words in parentheses.

1

Ruben plays the cymbals
loudly. (Ruben / loud)

2

_____ (Mel / beautiful)

3

_____ (Jen / quiet)

4

_____ (Joe / good)

5

_____ (Nina / bad)

6 Complete the sentences about you.

1 I _____ well.

2 I _____ quickly.

3 I _____ quietly.

7 Read and complete the sentences. Use the words in parentheses.

1 Dan plays the drums ___more loudly___ than Leah does (loudly).

2 Kim plays _____ Ed does (quickly).

3 Rosa _____ (better).

4 May _____ (beautifully).

5 Leah _____ (quietly).

8 Look at activity 7. Write the questions.

1 _Who plays the keyboard more slowly, Kim or Ed?_____
Ed does.

2 _____
May does.

3 _____
Sara does.

4 _____
Dan does.

5 _____
Rosa does.

9 **My World** Complete the sentences about you.

1 I play an instrument _____ than _____ does.

2 I run _____ than _____ does.

3 _____ does gymnastics _____ than I do.

4 _____ sings _____ than I do.

10 **Read the story again. Circle the correct words and then number.**

[ ] **a** It's an ocarina. **Jack / Ruby** tries to copy the tune.

[ ] **b** The yeti gives the children a **tablet / present**.

[1] **c** Jack, Ruby, and Sofia go back and find the **map** / **yeti** and the compass.

[ ] **d** The magic **tablet / ocarina** takes the children and the yeti away!

11 **Read and complete. Use the words in the box.**

> going ~~compass~~ ocarina slowly present yeti quickly

The children go back and get their map and ¹ ___compass___ . Then they see the

² _____ . He gives them a ³ _____ . It's an ⁴ _____ . Jack plays

the ocarina. He plays it ⁵ _____ and then again more ⁶ _____ . What's

happening? The children and the yeti are ⁷ _____ away.

12  **What can you do to show the value: persevere?**

1 <u>You can practice a musical instrument</u>

<u>every day.</u>

2 _____

_____

_____

3 _____

_____

_____

Story Value **41**

Skills: *Reading*

13 **Read Devon's interview. Complete with the correct form of the words in parentheses.**

▶ **Devon Lee** is a student at Oak School. He plays the violin in the school orchestra. He plays
¹ _beautifully_ (beautiful) now, but he didn't play very
² _____ (good) two years ago. We talked to Devon about it, and this is what he said.

▶ **Interviewer:** You play the violin very ³_____ (good), Devon. Was it always easy for you?

Devon: No, it wasn't. Two years ago, I played very ⁴_____ (bad).

▶ **Interviewer:** Really? Tell me about it.

Devon: The teacher asked me to play in a school concert when the other violin player moved to a different school. I was very worried because the other player played
⁵_____ (beautiful) than I did.

▶ **Interviewer:** What happened?

Devon: The kids in the orchestra helped me practice for two weeks. They were great. I played very ⁶_____ (good) at the concert. Those kids are my best friends now.

▶ **Interviewer:** Wow. That's a great story, Devon. We all know friends can be a big help!

14 **Look at activity 13. Read and write *true* or *false*.**

1 Devon is very good at playing the violin.   _true_
2 He always played the violin beautifully.   _____
3 The other violin player left Devon's school.   _____
4 The teacher helped Devon practice for two weeks.   _____
5 The children in the orchestra are now Devon's best friends. _____

15 **(TIP)** **We know adjectives describe nouns. Adverbs describe verbs.**
Adjective: John is *quick*.
Adverb: John runs *quickly*.
Read Devon's interview again. Circle three adverbs. Underline the verbs they describe.

Skills: *Writing*

16 (My World) **Make notes about someone who had a problem and a friend who helped.**

What was the person worried about?	How did the person's friend help?	What happened in the end?
_____	_____	_____
_____	_____	_____
_____	_____	_____
_____	_____	_____

17 (My World) **Write an interview about someone who solved a problem with a friend's help.**

▶ _____
_____

▶ _____
_____

▶ _____
_____

▶ _____
_____

▶ _____
_____

How do string instruments make high and low sounds?

1 Complete the sentences. Use the words in the box.

> high   ~~vibrate~~   low   quickly   lower   higher

1 A string instrument makes a sound when the strings ___vibrate___ .

2 When something vibrates slowly, it makes a _____ sound.

3 When something vibrates quickly, it makes a _____ sound.

4 When we play a guitar, the thick strings make a _____ sound than the thin strings.

5 Short strings vibrate more _____ than long strings.

6 Short strings make a _____ sound than long strings.

2 Look and answer the questions.

1 Who is making a high-pitched sound?

   ___Katie___

2 Why is the sound higher?
   Because the string is _____ .

3 Who is making a low-pitched sound?

   _____

4 Why is the sound lower?

   _____

   _____

5 Alice makes the guitar string tighter. What happens to the sound it makes?

   _____

   _____

3 In your notebook, design and write about a string instrument.

Evaluation

1 **Read and complete. Use the correct form of the words in the boxes.**

> quiet   bad   ~~good~~

My name is Linda, and I'm in the school band. I love music. I play the trombone and the trumpet. I play them very ¹_____well_____ . Everyone says I'm the best. I like to sing, too, but I sing ²_____ . Sometimes our teacher asks me to sing more

³_____ !

> quick   slow   bad

I'm not very sporty. I always run very ⁴_____ . I never win a race. My best friend, Nick, runs more ⁵_____ than I do. And I'm ⁶_____ at playing soccer than all the other kids in my class!

> quiet   quick   loud

I'm very friendly and talkative. I talk more ⁷_____ than any of my friends. Sometimes they ask me to slow down. I talk very ⁸_____ , too. I have to try to talk more ⁹_____ when I'm in the library or in class.

2 **Look at activity 1. Answer the questions.**

1 Does Linda play the trombone badly?   _No, she doesn't. She plays well._

2 What does Linda's teacher ask her to do?   _____

3 Does Linda run slowly?   _____

4 Who runs more quickly, Linda or Nick?   _____

5 Does Linda talk quietly and slowly?   _____

3 **Complete the sentences about this unit.**

✓ = I can ...   ✗ = I can't ...

☐ 1 ... name ten musical instruments.

☐ 2 ... talk about how someone does something.

☐ 3 ... compare how people do things.

☐ 4 ... talk about ways to persevere.

☐ 5 ... write an interview.

6 The part of this unit I found the most interesting was _____ .

Review Units 3 and 4

1 (Think) **Read and write the words. Then find and circle.**

1 This food is meat and vegetables on a stick.
You can eat it in Greece. _kebabs_

2 You hold this instrument in your hands.
Then you hit the two parts together.

_____

3 This is a Japanese dish with rice, fish,
and vegetables. _____

4 This instrument is like a piano, but it's
smaller. _____

5 Part of this dish is from the ocean. The other
part is made of potatoes. _____

6 You blow into this instrument. It's bigger
than a trumpet. _____

7 This food is popular in Thailand, China, and
Japan. It's like pasta. _____

8 You blow into this instrument. You hold it to
the side, not in front of you. _____

F	C	Y	M	B	A	L	S	X	D
I	W	L	W	T	G	E	H	D	U
S	O	H	Y	V	A	N	F	U	Y
H	P	Q	Z	L	S	O	L	G	Y
A	F	L	U	T	E	B	D	E	B
N	I	H	S	U	S	M	B	W	Y
D	O	K	E	Y	B	O	A	R	D
C	D	C	L	F	V	R	V	U	J
H	T	S	D	E	S	T	A	K	G
I	L	O	O	V	M	J	E	I	R
P	P	G	O	S	B	A	B	E	K
S	Q	H	N	F	W	H	P	Q	H

2 **Read and circle the correct answers.**

1 Jamie _____ Tom.
   a talks very quietly   **b** talks more quietly than   **c** talks quiet than

2 Our teacher _____ do our homework.
   a wanted us   **b** wants us to   **c** wants us

3 You play the saxophone _____ I do.
   a well than   **b** better than   **c** best than

4 Billie went to the supermarket _____ rice and fish.
   a to buy   **b** buy   **c** to bought

5 My sisters and I cooked the stew _____ .
   a very quickly   **b** very good   **c** very quick

3 **Read and complete the chart.**

John, Sarah, and Peter are in a band. Last night, they went to a restaurant to have dinner after the concert. They each had a different dish. Read the clues. Which instrument does each person play? What did each person eat?

Clues:
1　Peter ate Japanese food.
2　The keyboard player and the electric guitar player are boys.
3　The electric guitar player didn't eat sushi.
4　Sarah doesn't like rice.

	drums	electric guitar	keyboard	sushi	paella	tacos
Peter				✓		
Sarah						
John						

4 **Answer the questions about you.**

1　What's your favorite international food?

_____

2　What country is it from?

_____

3　What did your teacher want you to do in English class today?

_____

4　What did your friend want you to do yesterday?

_____

5　Which musical instrument would you like to learn to play?

_____

5 Now and then

1 Think Read and complete the sentences.

1 My dad reads the sports page in our city's __newspaper__ every day.

2 When I don't know a word, I usually look it up in a _____ .

3 My friends and I like to play _____ on my laptop after school.

4 My mom bought a new _____ for her e-reader.

5 I wrote a _____ to my aunt last week, because she doesn't have a computer.

2 Think Look and write the words in the chart.

Things that don't use electricity	Things that use electricity
a letter	_____
_____	_____
_____	_____

3 My World How often do you use the things in activities 1 and 2?

1 I never _____ .

2 I sometimes _____ .

3 _____ every day.

My picture dictionary → Go to page 89: Write the new words.

4 Look and complete the sentences with *could* or *couldn't*.

1 Mary ____could____ use an encyclopedia in 1970.

2 She _____ use the Internet in 1970.

3 She _____ read an e-book in 2010.

4 She _____ write a letter in 1970.

5 She _____ play online games in 1970.

5 Look at activity 4. Write sentences about Mary.

1 check the weather on a website / 2010
   Mary could check the weather on a website in 2010.

2 use an encyclopedia / 1970
   _____

3 send an email / 1970
   _____

4 use the Internet / 2010
   _____

5 read an e-book / 1970
   _____

6 Put the words in order.

1 an / My grandmother / couldn't / email / 1960. / send / in
   My grandmother couldn't send an email in 1960.

2 use / Your father / could / dictionary / young. / a / was / when / he
   _____

3 1995. / could / online / People / play / in / games
   _____

4 1980. / Sam's mother / read / e-books / in / couldn't
   _____

5 could / letters / 1970. / send / My grandfather / in
   _____

7 Look and answer the questions.

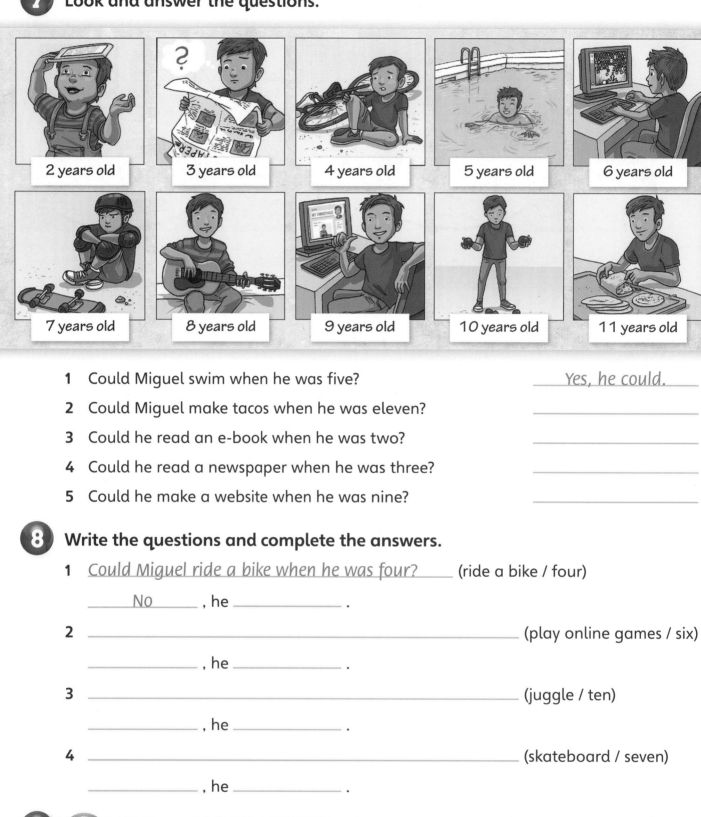

2 years old 3 years old 4 years old 5 years old 6 years old

7 years old 8 years old 9 years old 10 years old 11 years old

1 Could Miguel swim when he was five? _____Yes, he could._____

2 Could Miguel make tacos when he was eleven? _____

3 Could he read an e-book when he was two? _____

4 Could he read a newspaper when he was three? _____

5 Could he make a website when he was nine? _____

8 Write the questions and complete the answers.

1 _Could Miguel ride a bike when he was four?_____ (ride a bike / four)

   _____No_____ , he _____ .

2 _____ (play online games / six)

   _____ , he _____ .

3 _____ (juggle / ten)

   _____ , he _____ .

4 _____ (skateboard / seven)

   _____ , he _____ .

9 Write questions and answers about you.

1 _Could you read when you were five?_____ (read / five) _____

2 _____ (do cartwheels / nine) _____

10 **Read the story again. Match and then number.**

	The children find ____	**a** Ruby when she falls.
	Jack almost sits ____	**b** in the snow, and it's dangerous.
1	The children and the yeti climb _b_	**c** a letter when the snake leaves.
	The yeti catches ____	**d** on a snake in the cave.

11 **Read and complete. Use the words in the box.**

> rock   ~~mountains~~   Emoclew   cave   snowing   snake   Sofia   catches

The children and the yeti arrive in the ¹ _mountains_ . It's dangerous because it's

windy, and it's ² _____ . Ruby falls, but the yeti ³ _____ her. The

children follow the yeti into a ⁴ _____ . Jack thinks he's sitting down on a

⁵ _____ , but it's a ⁶ _____ ! When the snake goes away,

⁷ _____ sees a letter. The address is in ⁸ _____ . The children decide

to take the letter with them.

12   **What can you do to show the value: protect your friends?**

1 You can share your umbrella with your
friends when it rains.

2 _____

_____

3 _____

_____

Story Value **51**

Skills: *Reading*

13 **Read Robert's essay. Then look at the pictures and circle ☺ or ☹.**

Robert Simmons

The good and the bad of cell phones

Everyone loves new technology. People want to buy the newest computers, tablets, cell phones, and other gadgets. But our grandparents couldn't call or text their friends on cell phones. They couldn't look up information on computers or tablets. Are we happier now than they were then? I don't think so.

Cell phones are great. We can call our parents. We can call quickly for help in an emergency. We can text our friends and family. We can take photographs using our phones, so we don't have to carry a camera around. We can even go online with smartphones to get directions or find a good restaurant.

But cell phones aren't always great. We see people playing games or texting on their phones when they're with their family and friends. Why aren't they talking to each other? Some people drive and use their cell phones, and that's very dangerous. Some people walk and text at the same time. They sometimes fall and get hurt.

I think cell phones are great, but we have to be careful that we don't use them too much!

1 ☺ ☹   2 ☺ ☹   3 ☺ ☹   4 ☺ ☹

14 **Look at activity 13. Complete the sentences.**

1 Robert thinks we're not happier now <u>than our grandparents were then</u> .
2 We can use cell phones to call quickly _____ .
3 We can also use cell phones to find _____ .
4 Robert thinks people shouldn't play games or text when they're with
_____ .
5 He thinks driving and _____ .

15 **(TIP)** **We join two sentences together using *or*. We use *or* when there's a choice.**

You can read the article in the newspaper. You can read the article online. →
You can read the article in the newspaper *or* online.

Read Robert's essay again. Underline the sentences that use *or* and circle the two choices in each sentence.

Skills: *Writing*

16 Make notes about a kind of technology. Complete the chart about the good and bad things about it.

Kind of technology _____

Good	Bad
_____	_____
_____	_____
_____	_____

17 Write an essay about the good and bad things about a kind of technology.

Title: _____

_____
_____
_____
_____
_____
_____
_____
_____
_____
_____
_____
_____
_____
_____
_____
_____

What do primary sources tell us about life in the past?

1 Look and write the words under the pictures. Then check (✓) the primary sources from ancient Egypt.

> history book   ~~painting~~   board game   jewelry   tools   website   statue

 **a** ✓

painting

 **b**

_____

 **c**

_____

 **d**

_____

 **e**

_____

 **f** Ancient Egypt

_____

 **g**

_____

2 Look at activity 1. Read and write the letters.

1 This tells us that the Egyptians liked to play games.   `e`

2 This tells us that the Egyptians could make and play musical instruments.   ☐

3 This tells us that the Egyptians used tools for farming.   ☐

4 This tells us that the Egyptians wore beautiful objects.   ☐

5 This tells us that the Egyptians could make things from stone.   ☐

3 Imagine you see the primary sources from activity 1 in a museum. Choose two and write a question you can ask about each one.

1 _____

2 _____

Evaluation

1 **Read and complete with *could* or *couldn't*.**

My Uncle Bill is a smart man, but he isn't good at using technology. He tried to send an email, but he
¹___couldn't___ turn on the computer. He tried to text my aunt, but he ²_____ remember her cell phone number. He tried to read an e-book, but he ³_____ turn on his e-reader. He ⁴_____ play online games on his tablet because I helped him. "⁵_____ you use a computer when you were young?" I asked him. "No, Alice" he said. "We ⁶_____ use computers then because we didn't have them! But we ⁷_____ read newspapers, magazines, and send letters." Now I know why Uncle Bill isn't good at using technology!

2 **Look at activity 1. Answer the questions.**

1 Could Uncle Bill send an email? Why or why not?
  No, he couldn't. He couldn't turn on the computer.
2 Could he play online games? Why or why not?
  _____
3 Could he read an e-book? Why or why not?
  _____
4 Could he use a computer when he was young? Why or why not?
  _____

3 **Complete the sentences about this unit.**
  ✓ = I can …   ✗ = I can't …

  ☐ 1 … name ten kinds of technology.
  ☐ 2 … talk about what people *could* and *couldn't* do in the past.
  ☐ 3 … ask about what people *could* do in the past.
  ☐ 4 … say how to protect my friends.
  ☐ 5 … write an essay about the good and bad things about technology.
  6 My favorite part of this unit was _____ .

6 The environment

1 (Think) **Read and write the words. Then number the pictures.**

1 We use this to get hot water in our homes and sometimes to cook. _gas_

2 We use this for our lights, our computers, and many other things. _____

3 This is a hard, thick kind of paper. Boxes are made of this. _____

4 If we don't have this, we can't live. Plants and animals need it, too. _____

5 Drinks cans, parts of bicycles, and parts of planes are made of this. _____

6 This material can break easily. Bottles are sometimes made of this. _____

a

b
1

c

d

e

f

2 (Think) **Read and correct the underlined words.**

1 Newspapers and magazines are made of <u>cardboard</u>. _paper_

2 People can't use <u>wind power</u> in places that don't get much Sun. _____

3 Be careful with that bottle because it can break. It's made of <u>paper</u>. _____

4 My cousin lives close to a wind farm, so they use <u>solar power</u>, not gas. _____

5 Give the baby the <u>aluminum</u> cup, not the glass one. It's safer. _____

3 (My World) **What do you use that's made of plastic? What do you use that's made of aluminum?**

1 I use _____ and _____ . They're made of plastic.

2 _____ . They're made of aluminum.

My picture dictionary → Go to page 90: Write the new words.

4 Read and complete the interview with *should* or *shouldn't*.

Baytown School news

Keep Baytown green

Kevin is the leader of the Baytown School Environment Club. Our reporter, Jenny, asked Kevin for some ideas for keeping Baytown green.

Jenny: Kevin, tell us about some things young people should do to help keep Baytown green.

Kevin: There are a lot of things we should do. We ¹___should___ recycle plastic, aluminum, and paper. We ²_____ throw away newspapers, magazines, and cardboard. We ³_____ recycle them.

Jenny: What about trash? There are some things that we can't recycle.

Kevin: Yes, Jenny, that's right. We ⁴_____ make a lot of trash, and we ⁵_____ use a lot of plastic bags, because we can't recycle them.

Jenny: But we can reuse plastic bags.

Kevin: Yes, we ⁶_____ reuse plastic bags when we can.

Jenny: Let's talk about other things we can do at home.

Kevin: Well, we ⁷_____ use a lot of water. We ⁸_____ reuse rainwater in our yards.

Jenny: And we ⁹_____ waste electricity.

Kevin: Yes, we ¹⁰_____ turn off lights and computers when we aren't using them.

Jenny: How about outside of our homes?

Kevin: We ¹¹_____ ask our parents to drive us everywhere. We ¹²_____ walk or take the bus.

Jenny: Thank you for those great ideas, Kevin. Now let's all work hard to keep Baytown green!

5 Read and write *true* or *false*.

1 Kevin is the school newsletter reporter. _false_

2 The name of the club is Baytown Student Green Club. _____

3 There aren't many things young people can do to help the environment. _____

4 We should reuse plastic bags. _____

5 People shouldn't leave their computers on all the time. _____

6 People should travel by car a lot. _____

6 **World** **Which of Kevin's ideas do you think are the most important? Name two.**

1 I think we should _____ .

2 I think _____ .

7 Answer the questions. Then check (✓) the correct picture.

1 What should we do to save water?

We should collect rainwater for
our yards.

2 What should we do to save electricity?

_____

_____

3 What should we do to use less paper?

_____

_____

4 What should we do to reduce waste?

_____

_____

5 What should we do to save forests?

_____

_____

8 Complete the questions. Then circle the correct answers.

1 What _____ _should we do_ _____ to save energy?
   a We should use solar energy.   **b** We should throw our trash in the trash can.

2 What _____ save water?
   a We should recycle our cans.   **b** We should take showers, not baths.

3 What _____ paper?
   a We should write on both sides.   **b** We should use solar energy.

4 _____ waste?
   a We should reuse and recycle.   **b** We should do less homework.

5 _____ gas?
   a We should collect rainwater
   for our yards.   **b** We should use less hot water.

9 **Read the story again. Correct the sentences and then number.**

☐ **a** They follow the eagle to the rope mountain.

_____

☐ **b** Ruby sees that the bridge is new and tells Jack. They fix it.

_____

1 **c** The children pick up the ~~eagle~~ and take it with them.

The children pick up the trash and take it with them.

☐ **d** Jack helps the yeti, and it flies away.

_____

10 **Read and match the questions and answers.**

1 Did the children pick up the trash? ☐ c   a Yes, it is.

2 Who helped the eagle fly away? ☐   b They use a rope.

3 Where does the eagle take the children? ☐   c Yes, they did.

4 Is the bridge broken? ☐   d Jack did.

5 What do they use to fix it? ☐   e To the rope bridge.

11 **What can you do to show the value: reuse and recycle?**

1 _You can recycle newspapers and_

magazines.

2 _____

_____

3 _____

_____

Skills: *Reading*

12 Read Kerry's blog. Write the words under the pictures.

Go green with Kerry!

Hey, everybody! We all know we should reduce waste, reuse, and recycle. We know we shouldn't throw away old things if we can use them again. So I have a great message board you can make with ugly, old things. Here's what you need:

- A baking tray
- A hammer and a nail
- Wrapping paper
- Scissors
- Glue
- An empty can
- Bottle tops
- Notepaper
- Magnets

1. Ask your mom or dad to make a hole in one end of the baking tray with a hammer and a nail.
2. Measure and cut the wrapping paper to fit the baking tray. Glue the wrapping paper to the baking tray.
3. Measure and cut the wrapping paper to fit the can. Glue the wrapping paper to the can. Glue two magnets to the side of the can. Put the can on the baking tray for pens and pencils.
4. Glue magnets inside the bottle tops. Cover the front with notepaper. Put your board on the wall.

And there you have it! A beautiful new message board!
Visit my blog next time for ideas about saving energy.

1 **2** **3** **4** **5**

__magnets__   _____   _____   _____   _____

13 Look at activity 12. Put the sentences in order.

- [ ] **a** Stick wrapping paper on the baking tray and the can with glue.
- [ ] **b** Put your message board on the wall.
- [1] **c** Find an old baking tray and an aluminum can.
- [ ] **d** Put magnets on bottle tops and put them on the board.
- [ ] **e** Ask for help to make a hole in one end of the baking tray.

14 (TIP) **Antonyms are words that have opposite meanings.**

We had *good* weather on vacation. It was sunny every day.
We had *bad* weather on vacation. It rained every day.

Read Kerry's blog again. Circle the examples of antonyms.

Skills: *Writing*

15 (My World) **Make notes about something you can make by reusing old things.**

What can you make? _____

What do you need? _____

Circle the verbs you need to use in your writing: find, put, measure, cut, glue, make a hole, cover

Make notes about how you make it:
_____
_____
_____
_____
_____

16 (My World) **Write a blog about reusing things to make something new.**

_____
_____
_____
_____
_____
_____
_____
_____
_____
_____

What happens to our old glass bottles?

1 **Look and write the words under the pictures.**

furnace   recycling bin   green glass   clear glass   ~~melted glass~~   sand

a

b

c

melted glass

d

e

Glass bottles only

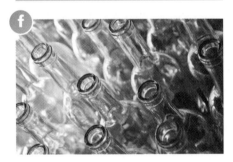
f

2 **Put the sentences in order.**

	a	A big truck comes and takes our old glass bottles away.
	b	They use the melted glass to make new bottles.
	c	The clear glass, green glass, and brown glass go in different groups.
1	d	We put our glass bottles in a recycling bin.
	e	Stores sell the recycled glass bottles.
	f	The glass melts.
	g	They put the glass and sand in a furnace.
	h	Machines break the glass and mix it with sand.

3 **How much glass, plastic, aluminum, and paper do you recycle each week? Make a bar chart.**

Evaluation

1 **Read and complete. Use the words in the box.**

shouldn't   cardboard   electricity   ~~aluminum~~   should   water   plastic   glass

Mandy's room is a mess! There are ¹ _aluminum_ cans on the desk. There are ² _____ bottles under the desk. There are ³ _____ bags under the bed. There are newspapers and magazines on the floor close to a big ⁴ _____ box. She should recycle the cans and bottles. She ⁵ _____ recycle the newspapers and magazines, too. Her computer and desk lamp are on. She should turn them off to save ⁶ _____ . Mandy is in the bathroom now. She is taking a long bath. She should take showers to save ⁷ _____ . And she ⁸ _____ be so messy!

2 **Read activity 1. Answer the questions.**

1 What should Mandy do with the cans and bottles?

She should recycle the cans and bottles.

2 What should Mandy do to save paper?

_____

3 What should Mandy do to save electricity?

_____

4 What should Mandy do to save water?

_____

3 **Complete the sentences about this unit.**

✓ = I can …   ✗ = I can't …

☐ **1** … name ten words about the environment.

☐ **2** … talk about what people *should* and *shouldn't* do.

☐ **3** … ask about what people *should* do.

☐ **4** … say how to reuse and recycle.

☐ **5** … write a blog about making something new from recycled things.

6 The part of this unit I found the most useful was _____ .

Review Units 5 and 6

1 Think **Read and complete the word puzzle.**

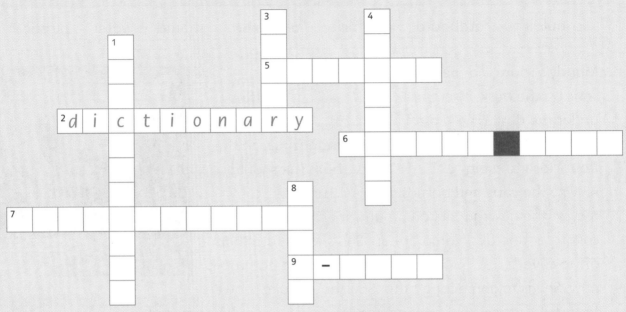

Across

2 This is a book of words.
5 A lot of bags are made from this.
6 We play this on the computer.
7 This is a big book with a lot of information.
9 We read this on a tablet or an e-reader.

Down

1 This gives us light at night.
3 This comes from trees.
4 This is what we use when we go online.
8 We need this to live.

2 **Read and circle the correct answers.**

1 Lisa couldn't _____ because it was broken.
   a reused the plastic bag   b reuse the plastic bag

2 Phillip shouldn't _____ .
   a play online games all day   b played online games all day

3 _____ you use a computer when you were young? No, I _____ .
   a Could, could   b Could, couldn't

4 What _____ we do to save paper? We _____ write on both sides.
   a should, should   b should, shouldn't

5 When my dad was at school, he _____ use an encyclopedia, but he _____ look for information on the Internet.
   a couldn't, couldn't   b could, couldn't

6 _____ you swim when you were six? No, but I _____ swim well now.
   a Could, couldn't   b Could, can

3 (Think) **Read and match the questions and answers.**

1 Could you read when you were three? `d`

2 My grandma doesn't have a computer, so I can't send her emails. ☐

3 Could you use a computer when you were six? ☐

4 I don't like going to bed early, but I'm always tired in the morning. ☐

5 Could you speak English when you were seven? ☐

6 I like playing sports outside in the summer, but I sometimes feel tired and get a headache. ☐

a No, I couldn't, but I could understand a little.

b You should drink a lot of water when you exercise.

c You should send her letters.

d No, I couldn't, but I liked looking at the pictures.

e You shouldn't play online games late at night.

f I could turn it on, but I couldn't use the Internet.

4 (My World) **Answer the questions about you.**

1 What technology do you use the most at home?

_____

2 Write two things you could do when you were four.

_____

_____

3 Write two things you couldn't do when you were six.

_____

_____

4 What kinds of energy do you use at home – electricity, gas, solar energy, or wind energy?

_____

5 What things do you usually recycle?

_____

6 What things do you usually reuse?

_____

1 (Think) **Read and write the words. Then number the pictures.**

1 We live on the planet _____Earth_____ . | r | t | E | h | a |

2 An _____ travels into space. | t | t | r | n | s | a | a | o | u |

3 There are eight _____ in our solar system. | e | a | t | l | p | s | n |

4 Astronauts travel to space in a _____ . | t | f | r | s | c | p | c | a | e | a |

5 The Sun is a big _____ . | r | t | a | s |

6 Neil Armstrong was the first man on _____ . | h | e | t | | o | M | n | o |

2 (Think) **Circle the one that doesn't belong.**

1 Earth   (spacecraft)   Mars
2 spacecraft   spacesuit   Earth
3 astronaut   planets   stars
4 the Moon   Mars   Earth
5 space station Mars   space laboratory

3 (My World) **What did you see in the sky last night? What didn't you see?**

1 I saw _____ .

2 I didn't see _____ .

My picture dictionary → Go to page 91: Write the new words.

4 **Look at Andy and Amy's calendar for next week. Complete the sentences.**

Monday	Tuesday	Wednesday	Thursday	Friday
Andy and Amy: ~~Go to the movies~~ Start space mission	Amy: Take photographs of Earth Andy: Clean up the spacecraft	~~Have a day off~~ Andy and Amy: Arrive at the space station	Andy: Do experiments in the space laboratory Amy: Work outside the space station	Amy: Clean the spacesuits Andy: Have an interview with NASA

1 Andy _____*isn't going to*_____ have an interview with NASA on Wednesday.
2 Amy _____ take photographs of Earth on Tuesday.
3 Andy _____ clean up the spacecraft on Friday.
4 Andy and Amy _____ arrive at the space station on Wednesday.

5 **Look at activity 4. Write the sentences.**

1 Andy / Tuesday
Andy's going to clean up the spacecraft on Tuesday. He isn't going to take photographs of Mars.

2 Amy / Thursday
_____

3 Andy and Amy / Monday
_____

4 Andy / Thursday
_____

5 Amy / Friday
_____

6   **Write two things you're going to do tomorrow and two things you aren't going to do.**

1 I'm going to _____ .
2 I'm _____ .
3 I'm not _____ .
4 _____

7 Put the words in order. Then circle the correct answers.

1 you / to / going / go / to / space camp? / Are
   Are you going to go to a space camp?
   a Yes, I do.   b (Yes, I am.)

2 going / he / do / is / at / What / to / the / space station?
   _____
   a He's going work outside.   b He's going to work outside.

3 to / the / climb / they / Are / going / Mars climbing wall?
   _____
   a No, they aren't.   b Yes, they did.

4 about / going / she / learn / Is / to / space missions?
   _____
   a Yes, she going to.   b Yes, she is.

5 going / astronauts? / to / Are / meet / you
   _____
   a No, you aren't.   b No, we aren't.

8 Look and answer the questions.

George   Abby   Sam   Christine

1 What's George going to do this weekend?
   He's going to bake a cake.

2 Is Abby going to bake a cake this weekend?
   _____

3 What's she going to do?
   _____

4 Is Sam going to play on the computer this weekend?
   _____

5 What's Christine going to do this weekend?
   _____

9 My World What are you going to do this weekend?

1 I'm _____ .

2 _____

10 (Think) **Read the story again. Circle the correct words and then number.**

☐ **a** They find a _____ with the letter *W* on it.
  a (wheel)　**b** map　　**c** tree

☐ **b** They find the _____ under the star and look under it.
  a tablet　**b** wheel　**c** tree

☐ **c** They all think and try to guess the _____ .
  a letter　**b** password　**c** number

[1] **d** The children look up at the _____ to find the brightest star.
  a city　　**b** sky　　**c** forest

11 **Circle the mistakes and write the correct words.**

1 Ruby is pointing to the (biggest) star in the sky.　　_brightest_

2 A red wheel is under the tree, coming out of the ground.　　_____

3 The children need the map to enter the city of Emoclew.　　_____

4 There are five blanks on the wheel for the other letters.　　_____

5 The children know that the letter C is important.　　_____

12 (My World) **When do you show the value: think logically?**

1 You think logically when you solve math problems.

2 _____
_____

3 _____
_____

Skills: *Reading*

13 **Read David's comic story. Circle the correct words.**

1 I'm going to be ¹**a spacesuit** / (**an astronaut**). I'm learning to fly a ²**spacecraft** / **space station** and float in zero gravity because soon I'm going to travel into space.

2 It's important to exercise in space, so I'm going to take a running machine. I'm ³**going** / **go** to take my dog Max and my laptop, too. I wonder, is there Internet in space?

3 Max and I ⁴**am** / **are** going to go for a walk on the Moon every day. We're going to get rock samples and then work in the ⁵**Earth** / **space** laboratory.

4 We're going to see big rocks ⁶**floating** / **walking** in space. We're going to break the biggest ⁷**rocks** / **stars** with lasers, so they can't come down to Earth. We're going to save our ⁸**Sun** / **planet**!

14 **Look at activity 13. Answer the questions.**

1 Is David going to be an astronaut?
  Yes, he is.

2 What's he doing to prepare?
  _____

3 What's he going to take?
  _____

4 Where are they going to work?
  _____

5 What are they going to do to the big rocks?
  _____

15 **(TIP)** **Some words are both verbs and nouns.**

The bird can *fly.* – There's a *fly* on the window.

I *walk* to school. – My mom and I go for a *walk* every evening.

My brother likes to *exercise.* – That's a difficult *exercise.*

Read David's comic story again. Find and circle *fly*, *exercise*, and *walk*.

Are they verbs or nouns?

Skills: *Writing*

16 (My World) Imagine you're going to travel to space. Make notes about your trip.

What are you going to do to prepare?	
What are you going to take?	
What are you going to do in space?	
How are you going to help the people on Earth or other planets?	

17 (My World) Write a comic story about your trip to space. Draw pictures.

How are the planets different?

1 Look and complete the words.

1 the S u n   2 _ e _ c _ r _   3 E _ _ t _

4 _ e _ u _   5 M _ _ s   6 _ u _ i _ e _

2 Read and write the words from activity 1.

1 It's the planet we live on. _____Earth_____

2 It's the biggest planet in our solar system. _____

3 It's the smallest planet in our solar system. _____

4 It's the planet closest to Earth. _____

5 It's one of the rock planets, and it's fourth in our solar system. _____

6 All the planets orbit it. _____

3 Write sentences about our solar system. Use the words in the box.

> is   has   moves   is made of   there are

1 _Jupiter is made of gas._

2 _____

3 _____

Evaluation

1 **Look at the timeline. Write sentences.**

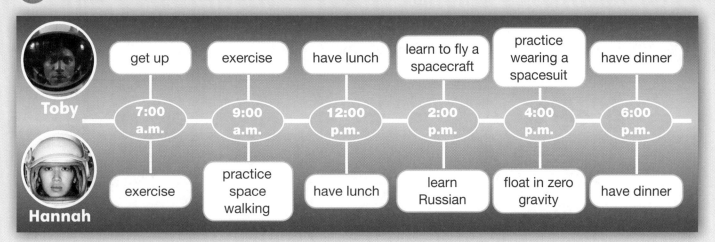

1 Toby / zero gravity / four o'clock
  Toby isn't going to float in zero
  gravity at four o'clock.

3 Toby and Hannah / lunch / twelve
  o'clock
  _____
  _____

2 Hannah / spacesuit / four o'clock
  _____
  _____

4 Hannah / Russian / six o'clock
  _____
  _____

2 **Look at activity 1. Answer the questions.**

1 Is Toby going to get up at 12:00 p.m.?   *No, he isn't.*

2 Is Toby going to exercise at 9:00 a.m.?   _____

3 Is Hannah going to learn Russian at 2:00 p.m.?   _____

4 Are Toby and Hannah going to have dinner at 8:00 p.m.?   _____

3 **Complete the sentences about this unit.**

✓ = I can …   ✗ = I can't …

☐ 1 … name ten words about space travel and space.

☐ 2 … talk about what people are *going to* do in the future.

☐ 3 … ask about what people are *going to* do in the future.

☐ 4 … talk about ways to think logically.

☐ 5 … write a comic story about space travel.

6 My favorite part of this unit was _____ .

1 Think **Look and complete the sentences.**

1 A ____pirate____ doesn't wear a mask.

2 My uncle is a very good _____ .

3 Rebecca's going to be a _____ in a carnival parade.

4 A _____ makes people laugh.

2 **Read and complete the sentences.**

1 When you put this on, no one can see your face. It's a ____mask____ .

2 This is an animal you can see and read about in story books. It's a _____ .

3 These are beautiful colorful lights in the dark sky. They're _____ .

4 There are fun, scary rides at this place. It's an _____ .

5 This is big and beautiful, and people stand on it in a parade. It's a _____ .

6 Dancers, clowns, and pirates wear this in a parade. It's a _____ .

My picture dictionary **Go to page 92: Write the new words.**

3 **Look and complete the sentences with *who*, *that*, or *where*.**

1 This is the park ____where____ we have
   a carnival in our town every year.

2 These are the musicians _____
   play the music.

3 These are the fireworks _____
   we see in the sky at night.

4 These are the floats _____
   are in the parade.

5 This is the street _____
   we watch the parade.

6 These are the dancers _____
   dance on the floats.

4 **Put the words in order.**

1 where / we / the amusement park / went on / rides. / This is
   This is the amusement park where we went on rides.

2 a pirate. / man / He's / who / the / dressed up / as
   _____

3 the most. / I / float / That's / that / like / the
   _____

4 there's / the town / where / This is / carnival / a big / every year.
   _____

5 the / She's / makes / woman / who / masks. / the
   _____

5 **Join the two sentences using *who*, *that*, or *where*.**

1 This is the clarinet. I played it in the talent show.
   This is the clarinet that I played in the talent show.

2 This is the town. There was a bad storm last night.
   _____

3 This is the astronaut. He's going to fly the spacecraft.
   _____

4 These are the dumplings. My mother cooked them for me.
   _____

5 It's the costume. My uncle made it for the parade.
   _____

6 Look and complete the questions and answers.

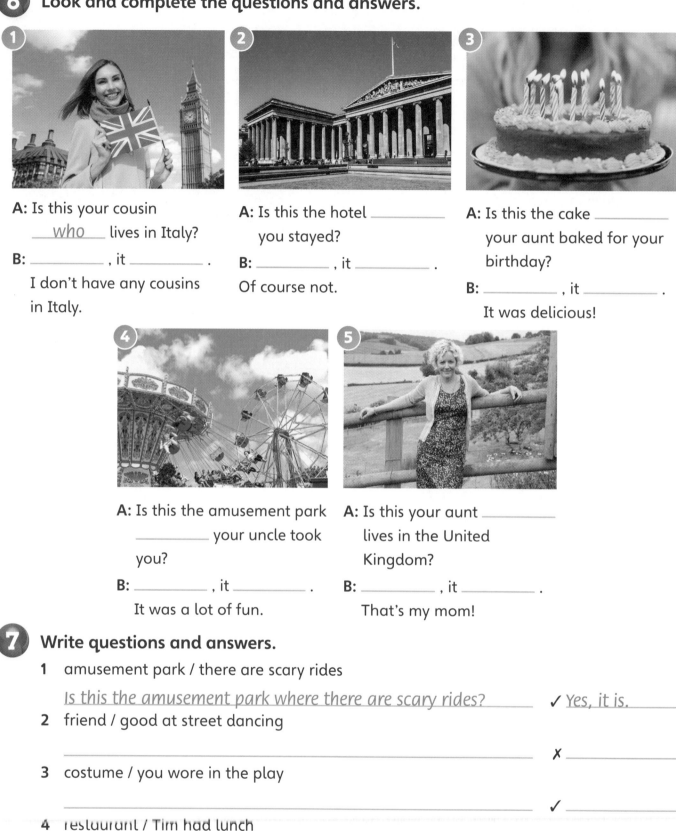

1

A: Is this your cousin ___who___ lives in Italy?

B: _____ , it _____ .
I don't have any cousins in Italy.

2

A: Is this the hotel _____ you stayed?

B: _____ , it _____ .
Of course not.

3

A: Is this the cake _____ your aunt baked for your birthday?

B: _____ , it _____ .
It was delicious!

4

A: Is this the amusement park _____ your uncle took you?

B: _____ , it _____ .
It was a lot of fun.

5

A: Is this your aunt _____ lives in the United Kingdom?

B: _____ , it _____ .
That's my mom!

7 Write questions and answers.

1 amusement park / there are scary rides

Is this the amusement park where there are scary rides? ✓ _Yes, it is._

2 friend / good at street dancing

_____ ✗ _____

3 costume / you wore in the play

_____ ✓ _____

4 restaurant / Tim had lunch

_____ ✓ _____

5 teacher / teaches you English

_____ ✗ _____

8 (Think) **Read the story again. Circle the correct words and then number.**

☐ **a** They have a lot of fun with the yetis at their **party / parade**.

☐ **b** The children find another word clue on the **street sign / door** and go back home.

☐ **c** They enter the competition, and their **password / game** wins!

1 **d** The children find the password (Welcome) / **Go home** and enter the yeti city.

9 **Read and complete. Use the words in the box.**

door   streets   ~~lost~~   competition   envelope   yeti   great   home   friends

When Ruby enters the password, the doors to the ¹_____lost_____ city open. The

²_____ is happy to be home. The yetis in the city welcome the children and the

yeti with a party. They all have a ³_____ time. When the children dance down

the ⁴_____ of the lost city, they see a sign that says Emoh Og. That's the street

on the ⁵_____ . They find number 3 and go in the open ⁶_____ .

They're ⁷_____ again, and the game is finished. Sofia enters the computer game

⁸_____ , and she wins! She shares the prize with her ⁹_____ .

10 (My World) **Write about two times when you showed the value: share success with your friends.**

1 *I shared success with my friends*
   when we won the soccer game.

2 _____
   _____

3 _____
   _____

Story   Value   **77**

Skills: *Reading*

11 **Read Tara's email. Then number the pictures.**

Hello Lucy,

    We're on vacation in the United States. We're staying with my cousins, Lily and John. They're the cousins who live in Florida. I'm having a great time. You can see the photographs that we took at Super Fun Park in this email. Super Fun Park is the place where we had a party for my birthday last Saturday. We had a great time. The rides were scary, but they were fun. My favorite ride was the roller coaster.

    We had hot dogs, burgers, and a big chocolate birthday cake for lunch. Then we went to the water park. It was a hot day, but the water was cold! John and I went down the water slide ten times! John can swim, but Lily can't, so we didn't stay there for a long time.

    That night, there was a parade with musicians and dancers and then amazing fireworks. I fell asleep in the car on the way home. I was tired, but I was happy. It was the best birthday ever!

See you next week.

Love,

Tara

1

12 **Look at activity 11. Circle the mistakes. Then write the sentences correctly.**

1 Tara is staying in Florida with her (friends,) Lily and John.

   Tara is staying with her cousins, Lily and John.

2 They celebrated Lily's birthday at Super Fun Park.

   _____

3 They had pizza, burgers, and chocolate cake for lunch.

   _____

4 They didn't stay long at the water park because John can't swim.

   _____

5 There was a carnival with dancers and musicians that night.

   _____

13 **(TIP)** **Use *but* to join two sentences together with opposite ideas.**

The box is big. It's not heavy. – The box is big, *but* it's not heavy.

You're happy. I'm not happy. – You're happy, *but* I'm not.

Read Tara's email again. Underline the sentences with *but*.

Skills: *Writing*

14   Make notes about a celebration or a visit to a theme park, an amusement park, or a carnival on the chart.

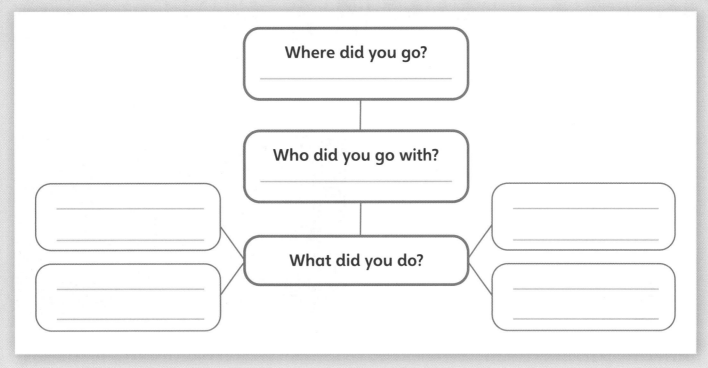

Where did you go?
_____

Who did you go with?
_____

What did you do?

_____
_____

_____
_____

_____
_____

_____
_____

15   Write an email about a celebration or a visit to a theme park, an amusement park, or a carnival.

Dear _____ ,

_____

_____

_____

_____

_____

_____

_____

Love,

_____

How do fireworks work?

1 Look and write the words from the box.

> fuse   gunpowder   ~~metal salts~~   lithium   sodium   copper

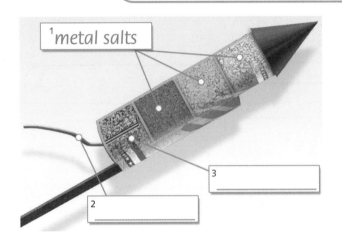

¹metal salts

3 _____

2 _____

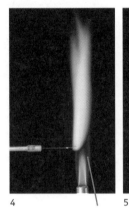

4 _____

5 _____

6 _____

2 Read and complete the sentences. Use the words in the box.

> metal salts   gas   ~~fuse~~   sound   air   gunpowder   explodes

Someone lights the
¹_____*fuse*_____ ,
so the
²_____
burns.

→

³_____
makes the
fireworks go up
into the
⁴_____ .

→

The gunpowder
⁵_____
and makes a loud
⁶_____ .

→

Different kinds of
⁷_____
inside the fireworks
make bright lights
in different colors.

3 Plan a celebration.

What are you going to celebrate?

_____

When and where are you going to have the celebration?

_____

What are you going to do?

_____

Evaluation

1 Read and complete.

1 This is the parade ¹ _that_ our town has every summer. And that's me! I'm Tim. I'm the boy ²_____ looks like a pirate. That's the costume ³_____ my mom made for me.

2 That's the place ⁴_____ they keep the floats. My favorite float is the one ⁵_____ looks like a dragon. Those dancers have masks ⁶_____ look beautiful.

3 These are the musicians ⁷_____ play the music. The man ⁸_____ plays the drum is my dad. That's the float ⁹_____ they always play.

4 After the parade, there's an amusement park ¹⁰_____ we can go on rides and buy delicious things to eat. This is also the place ¹¹_____ we have fireworks at night. It's great!

2 Look at activity 1. Answer the questions.

1 Is Tim the boy who is dressed up as a clown?   _No, he isn't._

2 Is he wearing a costume that his mom made?   _____

3 Is Tim's favorite float the one that looks like a pirate?   _____

4 Is the man who plays the drum Tim's uncle?   _____

3 Complete the sentences about this unit.

✓ = I can …   ✗ = I can't …

☐ **1** … name ten things you sometimes see at celebrations.

☐ **2** … talk about people, places, and things using *who*, *where*, and *that*.

☐ **3** … ask about people, places, and things using *who*, *where*, and *that*.

☐ **4** … talk about how you share success with your friends.

☐ **5** … write an email about a celebration at a fun place or event.

6 The part of this unit I found the most interesting was _____ .

Review Units 7 and 8

1 (Think) **Complete the sentences. Then find and circle the words.**

1 There are eight ____planets____ in our solar system.

2 There's a _____ with a parade and an amusement park in our town every year.

3 We can see many beautiful _____ on a clear, dark night.

4 That _____ has a red nose, wears a colorful costume, and is very funny.

5 It's not easy for an astronaut to learn how to fly a _____ .

6 In China, people think the _____ is a lucky animal.

7 An astronaut has to wear a _____ when he's outside the spacecraft.

8 If you wear a _____ , people aren't going to know who you are.

P	Q	C	L	O	C	K	K	M	V
L	W	A	Y	T	L	U	C	X	S
A	D	R	A	G	O	N	Z	V	P
N	A	N	F	B	W	G	M	E	A
E	N	I	K	C	N	F	I	R	C
T	C	V	H	A	F	Q	M	R	E
S	E	A	P	B	S	T	A	R	S
X	W	L	S	I	H	W	S	P	U
Z	D	A	S	T	O	N	K	J	I
S	P	A	C	E	C	R	A	F	T

2 **Complete the sentences. Use *going to*, *who*, *where*, or *that*.**

1 He's the astronaut ____who____ walked on the Moon.

2 The musicians aren't _____ play their instruments in the parade today.

3 That's the spacecraft _____ took the astronaut to Mars last year.

4 I'm _____ go to the carnival with my grandparents next weekend.

5 My friends are _____ eat space food at space camp.

6 That's the planet _____ they sent the *Curiosity* rover.

3 (Think) **Circle the one that doesn't belong.**

1 space station   spacecraft   space laboratory   the Moon

2 spacesuit   costume   Mars   mask

3 amusement park   musician   astronaut   dancer

4 amusement park   space laboratory   pirate   carnival

5 spacesuit   fireworks   stars   the Moon

82

4 **Think** **Read and complete the chart.**

Ruben, Evie, and Leo are going to go to their friend Marco's birthday party. They're going to wear costumes. Each person is going to wear a different costume. They each have a different birthday present for Marco. Read the clues. Which costume is each person going to wear? Which present is each person going to give Marco?

Clues:

1 Evie is going to wear a spacesuit.

2 Ruben's present for Marco is going to help him see when it's dark.

3 The astronaut isn't going to give Marco juggling balls.

4 The person who's going to wear a pirate costume isn't going to give Marco a flashlight.

	astronaut	pirate	clown	skateboard	flashlight	juggling balls
Ruben			✓			
Evie						
Leo						

 5 **Answer the questions about you.**

1 Would you like to be an astronaut? Why or why not?

_____

2 Would you like to go to space camp?

_____

3 Are you going to go to school tomorrow?

_____

4 What are you going to do for your next birthday?

_____

5 Would you like to go to a carnival? Why or why not?

_____

6 Is there an amusement park or a parade in your town?

_____

Seasons and weather

fall

blanket

do acrobatics

curry

clarinet

dictionary

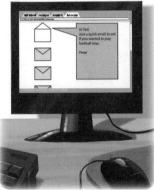

aluminum

astronaut

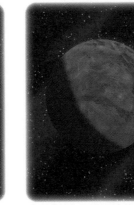

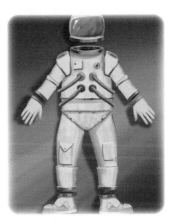

clown

Story fun

1 Who said it? Read and write the names.

Jack   Ruby   Sofia

1 _____Sofia_____   It's a wheel!

2 _____   Emoclew! We're in my game!

3 _____   Be careful, Ruby. It's dangerous.

4 _____   This is our egg!

5 _____   Oh, dear! There's a lot of lightning.

6 _____   I know! It's *Welcome! Emoclew* backwards!

7 _____   I can paddle.

8 _____   I think you have to copy the tune.

9 _____   Wait, Jack! The bridge is broken.

2   Look at the pictures and write the values.

Work together   Reuse and recycle   Persevere
~~Be resourceful~~   Eat healthy food   Protect your friends

1

Be resourceful

2

3

4

5

6

3 Complete the word puzzle with the clues from the story.

Across

1 Now it's time for you to look for a clue that you can cook. In a nest is a tasty treat, but someone else wants to eat.

2 Follow the footprints to a canoe. Inside it is your second clue. North, south, east or west. This item always knows where's best.

3 The sixth clue is the strongest bird, but you should help it - it is hurt. Rescue it from a rope trap, and find a short cut on the map.

4 The fifth clue is something you send to give your news to a friend. Pick this up and take it with you on your journey to Emoclew.

Down

5 Guess the password and all of you can enter the city of Emoclew.

6 The fourth clue is a present and a musical instrument. Listen carefully to a new friend, then play the tune to the end.

7 Do you want to find Emoclew? Here's the first thing you must do. Find a paper to show you the way. Some smart ants can help today.

8 Find the brightest star you can see. Under this star there is a tree. Look under the tree for your final clue. It is something round and blue.

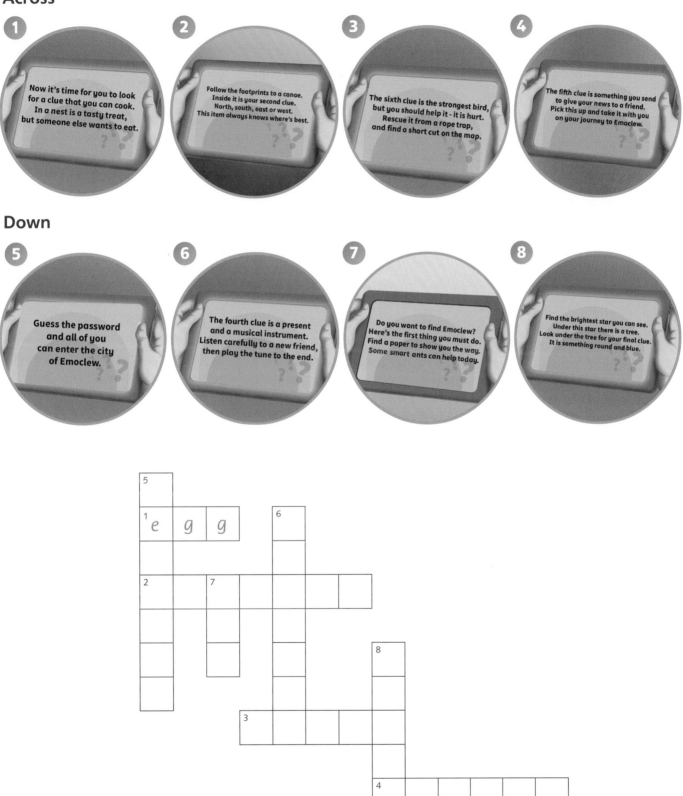